# RECUERDOS DE NUESTRO PASADO

Copyright 2018 by Angela Celaya, Sergio Guzmán, Jose Lovos, Gloria Revelo, & Erin Segal
Published by Thick Press

www.thickpress.com

ISBN 978-1-7320666-0-1

*Book design:* Omnivore, Inc.
*Storytelling:* Angela Celaya, Sergio Guzmán, Jose Lovos, Gloria Revelo
*Transcription:* Margarita Tobar Transcriptions and Translations
*Text:* Erin Segal
*Editing:* Davey Shlasko
*Printing:* Oddi Printing
*Paper:* Munken Print White, 115g/m$^2$ and UPM Finesse Silk 115g/m$^2$
*Typeface:* Freight Big, Mrs. Eaves, Archer, Caslon, Garamond and Arnhem Fine

The documents and photographic prints that appear as scanned images on pages 49–56 come from the personal collections of Angela Celaya, Sergio Guzmán, Jose Lovos, and Gloria Revelo. Erin Segal holds the copyright to the digital photos taken at the Senior Wellness Center. Any omissions or errors in copyright are inadvertent and will be corrected in subsequent editions.

RECUERDOS DE NUESTRO PASADO

*Angela Celaya, Sergio Guzmán, Jose Lovos, Gloria Revelo, & Erin Segal*

Angela: A mi hijo, Juan José Celaya.

Sergio: A quienes les interese, es regalado.

Jose: A la comunidad entera.

Gloria: A mis hijos, nietos, bisnietos, y a toda mi familia Revelo.

DEDICATORIAS

Erin: A nuestro *Grupo de Cuentos y Memorias*.

*Angela Celaya*     *Sergio Guzmán*

**JOSE:** *Gloria Revelo*

Jose Lovos is my name.
I was raised in El Salvador
by a mother and a father
but I always wanted to be outdoors,
up in the hills.

We lived in the village,
but I had no playmates.
I didn't go to school.
I never danced,
I never danced.

That's because
I spent my days
on a hilltop called La Pagona
where there were
lions, tigers,
and all sorts of mountain animals.

*Angela Celaya*   *Sergio Guzmán*

## GLORIA:

I was born on July 28th, 1935
in Las Lomitas
in San Miguel,
El Salvador.
And that's where we grew up,
all ten of us.

My parents never married
and they lived
their whole lives together
until my mama died when she was 100.

They lived a long, long time,
maybe because
they ate organic foods,
fruits,
chickens and eggs.
There was none of that fear
of thieves, those gangs
that go around
making trouble
these days.

I was the very first girl,
born after five boys.
They named me Gloria.
Gloria Emelina Revelo is my name.

## SERGIO:

My name is Sergio Guzmán Foley.
Guzmán from my mother,
Foley from my father.
My father is Irish,
my mother Honduran.

I was born in the
Republic of Honduras,
raised in the
Republic of El Salvador.
And I traveled to Honduras from time to time.

My parents never married.
My father left when I was two.
My mother raised me.

People ask: "Why didn't you put the Foley first?"
I reply: "Because my mother didn't marry him."

Time passed, and I wanted
to know everything.
I was itching to learn and
learn
and learn.

*Jose Lovos*   *Gloria Revelo*

# ANGELA: *Sergio Guzmán*

My name is Angela Celaya Cabrera.
I grew up in El Salvador
near the city, but back then
there was only primary school.
It was horrible,
the teachers were horrible,
not like today.

My mother had lots of children.
She said,
"I'm sending all my children to school,"
but some of them never learned anything;
they never knew what was A
and what was B.

I went to school, but I ignored the teachers.
I played with the boys, my cousins.
There was a long bench in the schoolroom
and we pushed and grabbed each other
until the one on the end
tumbled off.

*Jose Lovos*   *Gloria Revelo*

RECUERDOS DE NUESTRO PASADO

# II.

*Angela Celaya     Sergio Guzmán*

## JOSE: *Gloria Revelo*

I liked to work and sleep
in the hills
in La Pagona
where we had our camp.

The place where I slept was called
La Zapa
and in front, where the lion slept,
that was called
la Chilosa.

Because of the lion,
we hung the hammock up high.

From the hammock,
I watched boats in the sea
and in the summer
I saw shooting stars.

The lion and I never met.
I saw his tracks
by the natural rock pool
where he drank,
but I never met him.
He knew I was here, and I knew
he was there.

*Angela Celaya*  *Sergio Guzmán*

*Jose Lovos*

## GLORIA:

We worked in the countryside,
   in agriculture
growing yucca, corn, rice, beans—
we had everything.
Sugar cane and cotton, too.

We were happy.
Poor, but happy,
all ten of us
growing up with our parents.

*Angela Celaya*     **SERGIO:**

I kept hearing about
these mythical characters:
la Ziguanaba,
el Cipitío,
the Righteous Night Judge

and I said: "Why are they telling me these things?"

And then I began to think
it was because I was very naughty,
very nosy.
They wanted children to behave.
That's why they told me things like:
    "The Cipitío is going to get you."

Later, when I was in school,
they told us about
a writer named
Salvador Salazar Arrué—
Salarrué was his pen name.

He wrote about
myths
beliefs
and characters.

And that was how I came to understand that
some things are real,
others are not.

*Jose Lovos*  *Gloria Revelo*

# ANGELA: *Sergio Guzmán*

I left school to work.
At our house there were cattle and pork and
they killed the animals at three AM.
Pigs hanging,
and me with a big lit candle,
because they peeled everything off,
using boiling water,
leaving the skin clean.

I drew water from the well:
deep wells,
three lassos,
a wheel that turned when you pulled.
We used the water to fill up the
troughs for the animals.
We were always herding those animals
from place to place.

I left school again,
I worked more and more,
gathering cotton.
And then I worked like a man,
clearing brush with my machete.
I was always the first to finish,
famous with my machete in my hand.
The bossy men didn't like me—
"Get Angela Celaya out of here," they said.

*Jose Lovos*   *Gloria Revelo*

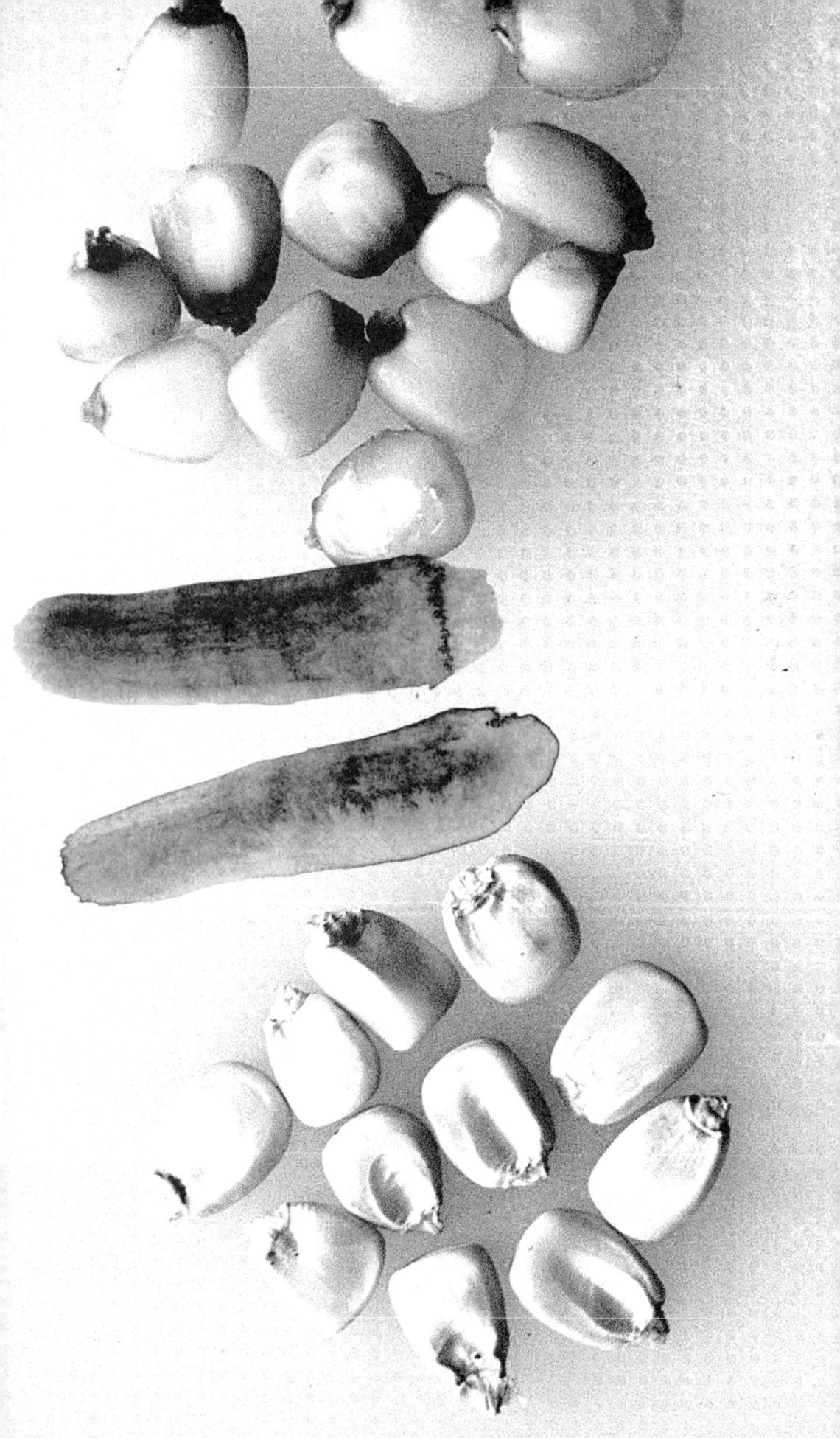

# III.

*Angela Celaya*  *Sergio Guzmán*

## JOSE: *Gloria Revelo*

And when I was ready to marry
I came down to
the village to
find a bride.

At 29, I bought
my first pair of shoes,
some dress clothes.
At 30, I married.

My wife was from my village
but she never knew me.

I used to walk past her house
in the morning in the dark,

and it was dark again
when I returned.

*Angela Celaya*   *Sergio Guzmán*

*Jose Lovos*

**GLORIA:**

I have always been a Catholic
and when I was 14 years old
I told my father that I wanted to gather
    together
a group of children
who had never seen the city.
They didn't know much about religion.
So with my father and my siblings
I put together catechism groups
and we brought 120 children
from the country
to the city.
We gave them First Communion.

*Angela Celaya*     **SERGIO:**

In 1944
I had finished secondary school
and my mind was agile
like a computer chip,
recording everything.
I haven't forgotten anything.

The war in El Salvador began with
the overthrow of a general who was the president;
his name was
Maximiliano Hernández Martínez.

Between then and now
so many ugly things have happened.

For 36 years
El Salvador was under military rule.
The political parties
cared only about power.
That's how the guerilla groups came about:
there was so much social injustice,
there were no schools.

If the son of a campesino succeeded
because he was bright,
they killed him;
they said he was a Communist.

*Jose Lovos*   *Gloria Revelo*

## SERGIO:

If a worker succeeded,
they killed him;
they said he was a Communist.
University students, too.

In the peace accords
at the end of the war,
the military agreed to reduce its numbers
by a third,
to 30,000 armed men,
and the guerillas had to disappear.

All those people—
those guerrilla fighters, those army soldiers—
those are the people who formed gangs:

M13,
M18.

I didn't want to talk about all this
but I know it well.
I lived there. I
remember
everything.

*Jose Lovos*   *Gloria Revelo*

# ANGELA: *Sergio Guzmán*

There was a boyfriend
but I didn't like him.
I was like a man.
I wanted to go wherever I felt like going:
a dance one day,
a funeral another.

When I was 24
riding on a horse
him in front, me behind
he grabbed me
and there was a fight
and I fell off and fainted
and he fell on top of me
and when I woke up, he said,
"I've chosen you to be the woman of my house"
and he took me to a village far away
and kept me in a house
with his mother
with no money,
only food.
I was pregnant.

I woke up early one day.
The only thing I took from that house was my bed sheet,
and I went to San Miguel.

*Jose Lovos*  *Gloria Revelo*

# IV.

RECUERDOS DE NUESTRO PASADO

*Angela Celaya*  *Sergio Guzmán*

## JOSE: *Gloria Revelo*

It was becoming difficult to live in the countryside
because of a group called the guerilla.
The guerilla did so many bad things.

A group called
*Legión de María Caballeros de Cristo Rey*
got me into religion.
They brought me to an American Center
and made me a commander.
Me! An illiterate commander!

In the countryside
in a rustic shrine,
with women and children gathered round,
I taught catechism
and reading and writing
I, who didn't know how to read or write!

*Angela Celaya*   *Sergio Guzmán*

*Jose Lovos*

## GLORIA:

When I was 20, I had a boyfriend.
We never married.
I became a single mother.

I had two children and
I took in a baby
a year and a half old,
the same age as my daughter.
I raised the girls as if they were twins.

When my youngest was just
a few days old
the father left,
that womanizer.

I never took him back
because I was bitter—
very, very bitter.

My parents helped me
and I worked and
I raised my children.

*Angela Celaya*  **SERGIO:**

In 1956 I had the opportunity to
join a project of the
*Oficinas Sanitarias Panamericanas*
in El Salvador
to eradicate malaria,
and I accepted.

I worked with them for 14 years.
I learned to draw plans to scale,
I learned engineering.

And then the
*Oficinas Sanitarias Panamericanas*
sent us to a laboratory
so we could study
the customs
and habits of the mosquito.
When they bite
when they don't bite
whether they bite people or animals.

And I went with them
to the swamps and rivers.
I worked from six in the morning until six at night.
I let the mosquitos
bite my skin
as if I were a guinea pig
and I learned so many things.
Our boss was a Brazilian doctor
named
René G. Rachou.
He showed me everything.

*Jose Lovos*   *Gloria Revelo*

## ANGELA: *Sergio Guzmán*

I was working in San Miguel
and I had my baby in the hospital.
I still have the scars from my baby
because I don't have enough space to get a baby out.
The child didn't come out.
I labored all day,
so much pain.
Finally the baby came out.
I was all groggy with anesthesia.
He was a boy.

My baby died
when he was eight months old.

*Jose Lovos*   *Gloria Revelo*

*Jose Lovos is my name.*

*Gloria Emelina Revelo is my name.*

*My name is Sergio Guzmán Foley.*

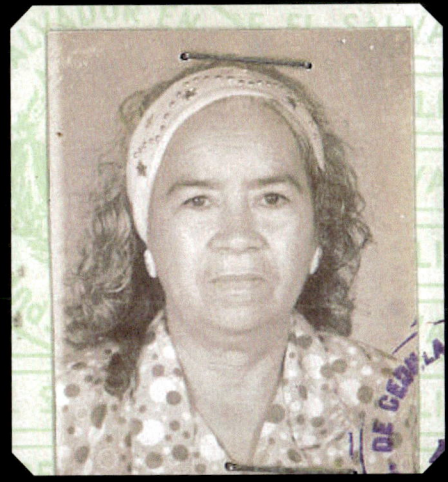

*My name is Angela Celaya Cabrera.*

*We worked in the countryside, in agriculture
growing yucca, corn, rice, beans—*

*and reading and writing
I, who didn't know how to read or write!*

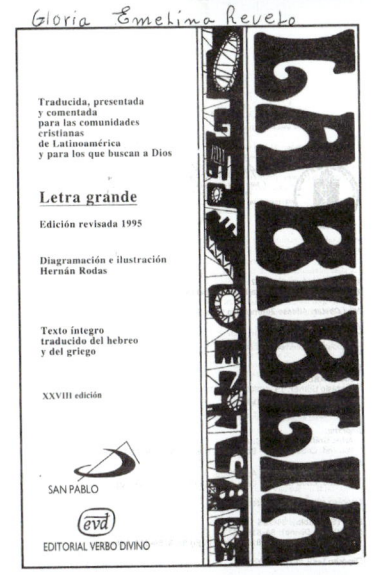

*I have always been a Catholic*

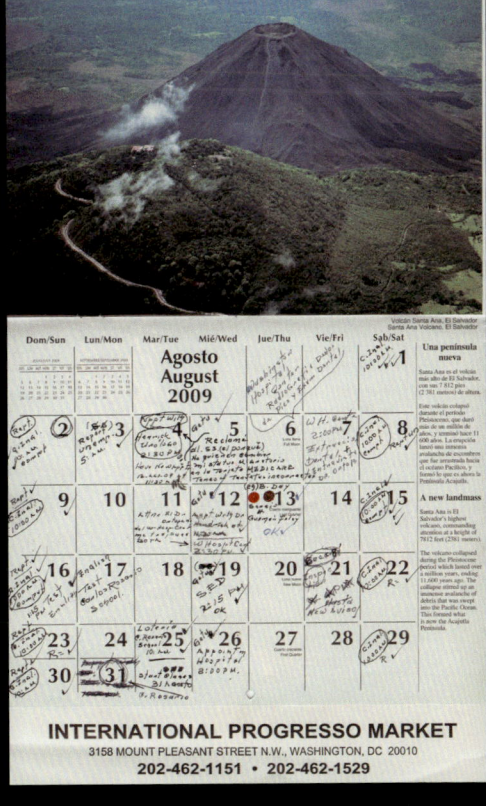

*And I went with them
to the swamps and rivers.*

RECUERDOS DE NUESTRO PASADO

Estatura 1.53 (Centímetros) Peso 57 (Kilogramos)

Color de la piel trigueña

Color de los ojos café

Pelo cano

Señales Especiales

Impresiones Digitales

DEPTO. DE CEDULA DE IDENTIDAD PERSONAL San Miguel

6 REPUBLICA DE EL SALVADOR 7

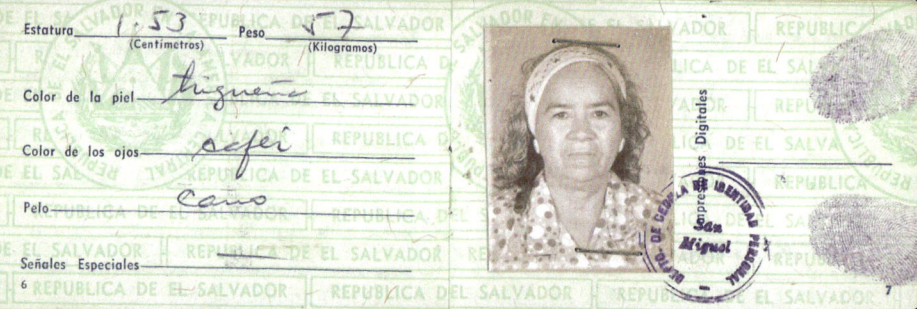

*and I went to San Miguel.*

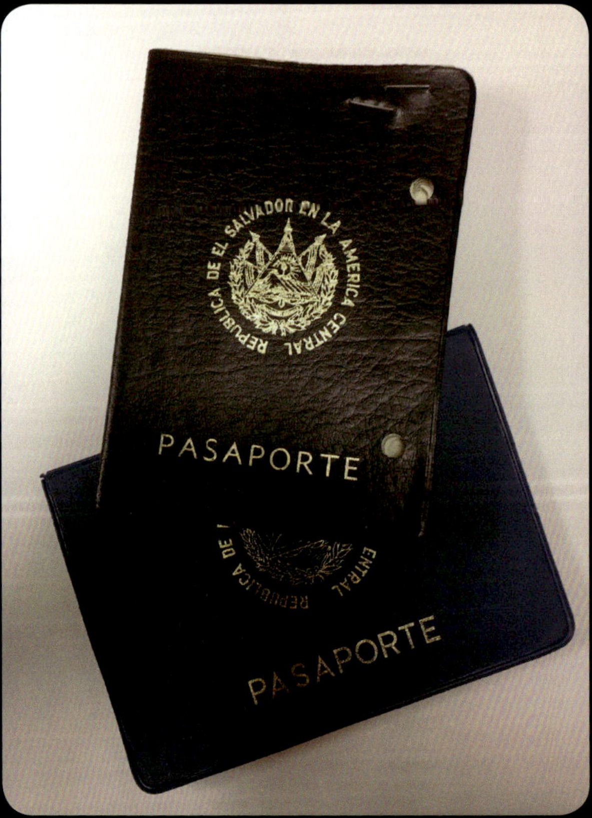


*I told a lawyer*

*So they gave it to me,*
*that diplomatic visa.*

*taking care of all those places*
*filled with Americans,*
*just Americans.*

*I've had such magnificent bosses.*

*I also know Virginia, Maryland, other states, too.*

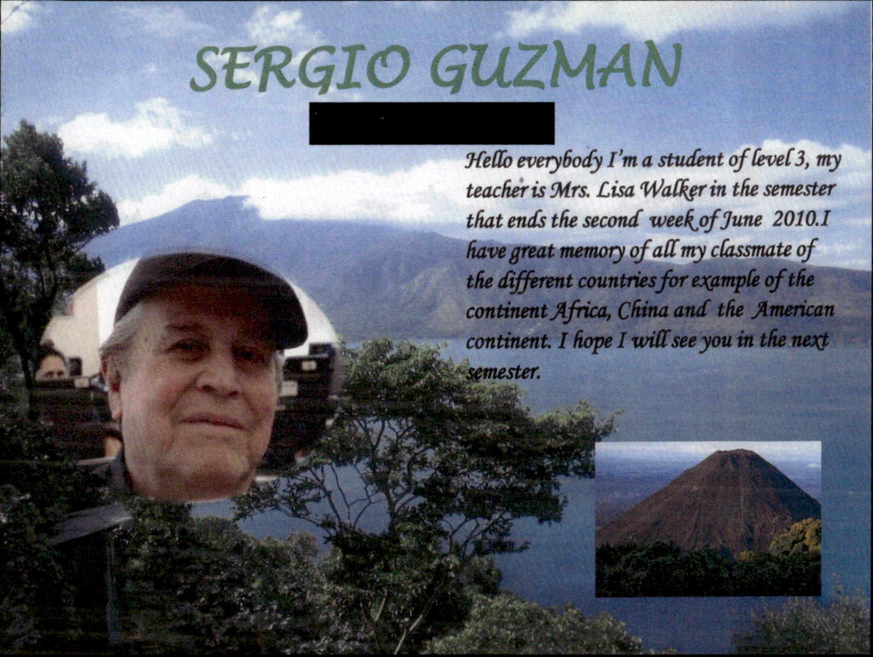

# SERGIO GUZMAN

*Hello everybody I'm a student of level 3, my teacher is Mrs. Lisa Walker in the semester that ends the second week of June 2010. I have great memory of all my classmate of the different countries for example of the continent Africa, China and the American continent. I hope I will see you in the next semester.*

*Here I studied at a school called Carlos Rosario.*

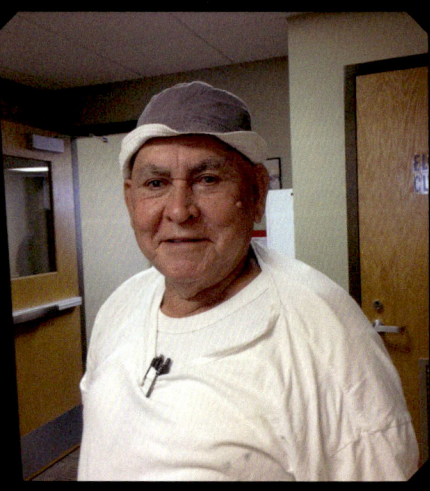

*Jose Lovos is my name.*

*Gloria Emelina Revelo is my name.*

*My name is Sergio Guzmán Foley.*

*My name is Angela Celaya Cabrera.*

*Angela Celaya*   *Sergio Guzmán*

JOSE: *Gloria Revelo*

I was never bad with anybody
but I was a commander
and the guerrillas were ordering that commanders
 be killed
so I decided it was better to come here,
to the United States.

I came and
here I am.

I told a lawyer,
the lawyer arranged the paperwork.

*Angela Celaya*   *Sergio Guzmán*

*Jose Lovos*

## GLORIA:

I was working a lot over there
and one day
this cousin, Israel Aguilar,
sent a diplomatic visa for a sister-in-law.
But she didn't have anybody to care for
   her children.
So they gave it to me,
that diplomatic visa.

*Angela Celaya*    **SERGIO:**

The Brazilian doctor died,
the project was over,
and I started working in commerce,
as a sales agent for a factory in Los Angeles.

I traveled all over El Salvador
and I began to see dead people in the streets
and it was scaring me
because I saw horrors, murders
and I can't describe it
because I don't like to talk about it.

I started feeling hatred
because they assaulted me and robbed all the
 product from the sale I had made
and then I wasn't afraid anymore.

I came to this country because they tried to kill me.
It wasn't because I belonged to a political party,
not at all.
I know now—and I knew then—that for good
 or for bad
it had to end
at one moment or another.

I came here because
if I had stayed there
they would have killed me.

*Jose Lovos*  *Gloria Revelo*

# ANGELA: *Sergio Guzmán*

I buried my son.
I lived with my sister for two more years,
and then I went to the capital to look for work.

I worked for a good woman,
cleaning.
I had to learn to cook differently than I cooked
in the country.

That's how I earned the money to come here.

I'm not wet.
The wetbacks are the ones who crossed the river.
I just walked.
I was an alambrista,
a wire crosser.

I crossed the wire
with a coyote and many, many women.

They say everybody is abused by the coyote,
that's a lie.

Peacefully, all of us walking
through the desert, over hills.
When Immigration came—
big headlights on the truck,
the airplane overhead—
we hid underneath some
prickly bushes.

I'm not wet.
I was a wire crosser.

*Jose Lovos*     *Gloria Revelo*

RECUERDOS DE NUESTRO PASADO

# VI.

RECUERDOS DE NUESTRO PASADO

*Angela Celaya*   *Sergio Guzmán*

**JOSE:** *Gloria Revelo*

I came straight to Washington
because my brother lived here.
I worked for a lady in Alexandria
who treats me like a son.
She speaks twelve languages.
She worked for the government.

I worked Monday to Saturday
from nine in the morning
until ten at night.
On Sundays
I washed my clothes.
And then all over again.

In 1977, I got into landscaping.

*Angela Celaya*   *Sergio Guzmán*

*Jose Lovos*

## GLORIA:

After three years
I was a resident.
(Now I'm a citizen!)
By my fourth year,
I had all my children with me.

I had already told them what life was like.

They worked,
they married,
they had their children.

My daughter died when she was almost 56.
My son died at 56, too.

So now I only have the other daughter,
the grandchildren,
and the daughter-in-law,
it's as if she were my daughter.
And I've spent almost 30 years
raising the grandchildren and the
 great-grandchildren.

*Angela Celaya*     **SERGIO:**

I know Texas,
New Mexico, Arizona, Los Angeles.
It was from Los Angeles
that I came here.
I also know Virginia, Maryland,
other states, too.

I appreciate this country
because it is a very generous country.

People come here to
make something of themselves,
not to do bad things.

There are immigrants here
from all over the world,
not only Latin America.

*Jose Lovos*     *Gloria Revelo*

# ANGELA: *Sergio Guzmán*

I worked for a Mexican family in Los Angeles.
I've had such magnificent bosses.

For seven years I cared for
the little girl.

She called me Tata.

After I moved to Washington,
I went back to Los Angeles
to visit the little girl.
She thought I was there to stay.
She hid under the bed.
She wouldn't eat.

She still comes to see me, mi bodoquito.
She came for my birthday,
brought me a mountain of stuff.

*Jose Lovos*   *Gloria Revelo*

# VII

RECUERDOS DE NUESTRO PASADO

*Angela Celaya*     *Sergio Guzmán*

## JOSE: *Gloria Revelo*

I worked at the Basilica
earning $2.70 per hour.
"What do you need?" they asked.
"Two assistants and two clippers," I said.
They sent me to International Drive,
and a place in Maryland
and Holy Cross
and Leisure World.
All over Connecticut Avenue.
To Skylight:
12 buildings, 30 floors.

So many places!
An illiterate guy
taking care of all those places
filled with Americans,
just Americans.

The boss was American.
He didn't speak Spanish,
then he learned.
He told me to clean over here and over there
and he liked what I did.
I worked fast.
When he arrived in the morning,
I was already there.
20 years, he never scolded me.
He was happy with me,
and I was happy with him.

Cuban cigars killed him.
Thank God I've taken care of myself.

*Angela Celaya*   *Sergio Guzmán*

*Jose Lovos*

## GLORIA:

When I first came here,
the bus cost 25 cents,
then it went up to 40 cents.
With $50 you could fill up the shopping cart
with enough food to last a week.
Now it costs $300 to buy what you bought then.
Everything changed.
Now you make more money.
When I came, we earned very little,
just $35 dollars a day.

I worked for the same family
for 25 years,
two girls.
Such a nice family.

The parents left me some money in their will
$40,000.
I said to my kids:
"Let's buy a house."
And that's how the children have always lived
  with me,
and the grandchildren, too.

Our family is close,
very close.

*Angela Celaya*  **SERGIO:**

I'm very happy because when
I was educated in El Salvador
they didn't know about computers and
I didn't learn much English.
Here I studied at a school called Carlos Rosario.
I reached the fifth level.
I learned Basic Computer:
Microsoft Word,
Microsoft Publisher,
Excel, all that.
I have a gift for computers.

*Jose Lovos*  *Gloria Revelo*

# ANGELA: *Sergio Guzmán*

My boss had lots of guys coming in
and out of the house.
One of them said, "Hey Angela,
You're not looking for a husband?"
I looked at him and I said,
"They sent me here because I killed two men.
Do you want to be the third?"

When I told my boss
he burst out laughing.

*Jose Lovos*   *Gloria Revelo*

# VIII.

RECUERDOS DE NUESTRO PASADO

*Angela Celaya*   *Sergio Guzmán*

## JOSE: *Gloria Revelo*

My friend
worked
in the government,
and she brought me to
meetings with professionals,
just professionals.

I was there at the Hilton with Marion Barry;
I rocked Marion Barry's baby,
the boy who died from drugs.

I dined in the basements
of all the museums
with Wonder Woman and her friends,
all professionals—
and me, an illiterate guy!

*Angela Celaya*   *Sergio Guzmán*

## GLORIA:

I give advice
to young women.
I tell them,
"Look, I'm a single mother and I never got married,"
and this thing about abandoning children—
I tell them they must raise their children,
they must work hard,
give them love,
care for them,
teach them,
speak kindly to them.
I tell single mothers to think it over.

I never studied anything,
but my father always guided us.
I give good advice.
My granddaughters are studying psychology
because I advised them well.

**SERGIO:**

That's what I can tell you about my life
from my childhood to today.
I thank you
for giving me the opportunity to talk about these things.
I appreciate it so much.

*Jose Lovos*     *Gloria Revelo*

## ANGELA: *Sergio Guzmán*

Most of my family is dead, the little family there is.

I always sent money:
sending money, sending money.

When my mother died, I couldn't go
to El Salvador
because my residency was in process.

Now I am a citizen.

*Jose Lovos*  *Gloria Revelo*

# IX.

*Angela Celaya*     *Sergio Guzmán*

## JOSE: *Gloria Revelo*

I have six boys and four girls,
the last two born in Washington.

Two of my girls are happy with their dad—
I am their love; they adore me.

I don't understand my family very well.

But I don't complain because
I have the house.
I'm a child of poverty, yet I've always lived well.

You need to do the right thing,
do no harm.
I say: you can do something bad
unintentionally,
because of ignorance, but intentionally—
that's no good,
because the refrain says:
*El que mal anda, mal termina.*
Because that's how we are.
Tomorrow we won't exist,
this life goes away, it ends.
That's how it is.

*Angela Celaya*   *Sergio Guzmán*

## GLORIA:

And that's my story
and here I've stayed.
My children died,
my sister, too.
They're buried here, at peace,
and here I'll stay until God wants me to give
Him my life.

I'll keep on fighting,
trying hard.

And here I am,
together with others in this Senior Center.
I like this place.
I do my exercises and
I have friends.
I like dancing, doing shows.
I spend time with everybody here.
We've shared all these stories
and we've learned to know each other better.

My daughter has two children who
have graduated from the university,
one who is studying.
And we live
with the great-grandchildren, too.
I have my children
and we all live together.

**SERGIO:**

I have nothing else to add
because right now
I live in this country

and I'm thinking
I won't stay here any longer.
I'm thinking I might
go to Ireland
to live.

There would be another world
over there, another universe,
right?

*Jose Lovos*   *Gloria Revelo*

**ANGELA:** *Sergio Guzmán*

You know,
since I've come to this country
I've been at peace.

# ERIN:

In late 2016, at Mary's Center's Bernice Fonteneau Senior Wellness Center in Washington, DC, I facilitated our Monday morning *Grupo de Cuentos y Memorias*. The four of you—Jose, Gloria, Sergio, and Angela—formed the group's core. Other participants drifted in and out.

The five of us first met the previous year, when I came to the Center to facilitate a dialogic discussion group about wellness. I am a social worker who always tries to think about my practice in terms of groups and communities, not just individuals. At the time, I hoped our discussions about wellness might result in community organizing. But whenever I mentioned "action," you told me you wanted to relax. You had worked hard for many years. The time had come to enjoy your old age, you said. You visited the Center to socialize. To exercise. To use computers. To make handicrafts.

I know nothing about handicrafts, but I have experience with interviewing and writing, so the Center staff suggested that I offer a memoir-making group. The next group I offered was our *Grupo de Cuentos y Memorias*.

It was important to me that I offer a memoir *group*, not a memoir class. Being a group worker means that I value group process and mutual support. I wanted our group to be more about sharing stories and memories, less about producing texts. I reasoned that the memoir-writing part should come later, in individual sessions with me, after we'd all had a chance to tell our stories aloud. The Center liked that plan, and you did, too.

During our group sessions, I sometimes shared my own stories. But mostly I listened, straining to understand your words, as Spanish is not my first language. I offered prompts. I noted commonalities. I kept time. I offered reminders about respecting difference. I also tried to make sure everybody had space to talk. Those are the kinds of things group workers do.

## ERIN:

Even though I used group work skills, it never felt like I was practicing social work *on* you. We were group members sharing stories, and my role was to keep us on task.

After four months passed, I sat down individually with each of you and recorded thirty minutes of storytelling. During those individual sessions, we started with childhood and ended with the present day. Sometimes, I asked questions. Sometimes, I invited you to add stories I remembered from group sessions.

I sent the recordings to a professional bilingual transcriptionist who transcribed them. Reading the transcripts was helpful for me because I read Spanish better than I understand spoken Spanish.

I turned the transcripts into written Spanish-language memoirs. I reordered some of the sentences, but I was very careful not to change your words. We met again, each of you individually with me, and I read the edited transcripts aloud to make sure everything was just right. I think you liked hearing your words read back to you. You listened very carefully. Sometimes you interrupted me, expanding on a story. You often used the very same words that appeared later in the transcript. People tend to tell the same stories over and over again.

You showed me photos, too. With my phone, I snapped photos of your photos so we could include them in your memoirs.

After spending hours editing the transcripts, I understand your lives much better than I had during the group sessions. It makes me wish I could transcribe everything anybody ever told me. Conversations often pass me by.

I tried to translate your memoirs into English, but my translations never sounded right. They never sounded like you. I knew other people would be interested in hearing your stories, but the translated memoirs were very long. It seemed to me that when I presented them individually, your stories lost the power of being grouped with other stories.

One day, I had a scheduled appointment with Sergio.

# ERIN:

When I called to confirm, he told me the Center was closed for Emancipation Day, a DC holiday. My kids were in school. Suddenly, I had nothing to do, nowhere to be.

I sat down on the rug and began to write.

For me, this was unusual. I *aspire* to sit down to write, but most days I don't. The tug of my to-do list is very powerful.

I started with Jose's description of La Pagona. Without thinking, I knew Gloria's story should begin next, then Sergio's, then Angela's. I constantly referred back to your words, reading them until I had practically memorized them. I wasn't exactly translating the texts. This multi-vocal English language text came from your words and your experiences, but it was mine, too. I chose the pieces I liked best. I decided how to arrange them. I tried to stay faithful to your stories, but in the end, I tended to emphasize the things that interest me most: family relationships, farm life, identity, and how people meet their material needs. I lingered on parts that delighted me because they were un-familiar or hard to believe. I tried not to shy away from pieces that were upsetting. I ordered events chronologically. I didn't always seek parallels between experiences, but each section emerged in relation to the other sections.

The emerging text moved me; to my ears, it sounded gorgeous. Even though it was in English, it sounded so much like the Jose, Gloria, Sergio and Angela I know. It spoke to me; it spoke for itself. I thought we might turn it into a performance or a book that others could hold and read and learn from. But then I worried about taking your stories and making them into something *I* valued. That's what colonizers do, and I wanted to be sure I was doing something different.

I stopped worrying when I remembered that we are always borrowing from each other, absorbing each other, taking each other in. You have given me voice, and I have found a forum for you to share pieces of your lives, and, as Gloria says, we've shared so much together.

# ERIN:

So, finally, I screwed up the courage to ask, "What do you think about turning your stories, our story, into a performance? Or perhaps a book? Or both?"

You said book. A performance is fleeting; a book is an object that might outlast us all. You said you wanted the book to be in English, not Spanish, because more people in the United States would be able to read it. Jose worried that it was too much work for me; Gloria assured Jose that I, too, benefit from this work.

You decided we would have a party when the book was complete.

And so, once again, we met individually. I read the English verses I had produced using your words, following each reading with a line-by-line verbal translation. Together, we made clarifications. In some cases, we removed parts that worried us—because they might endanger you or offend other people, living or dead.

To turn the text into a book, we worked with a designer I know, my childhood friend, Julie Cho. She and I conceived of this project as a small, limited-edition book. But we didn't know any presses that publish collaborative projects like this one.

Inspiration struck: Julie and I should start a small press, which could publish this project as its first book! Starting a press had never been in my plans; it's funny how life unfolds. You know that, of course.

You were generous about entrusting our project to the new press. You understand that our book is interesting to people who want to experience a mosaic about Americans raised in El Salvador in the 1930s. I hope you understand that this section might be valuable to social workers trying to expand their repertoires beyond assessment and treatment. It might be valuable to artists interested in social practice. Thank you for letting me include it.

So now the five of us have a book! And Julie and I have a press! Who knew? This is what dialogic work is all about. I am so grateful to have the opportunity to do group work spaciously, slowly, seeing what emerges.

# ERIN:

I hope this book will help people to see the social value of sharing stories and making beautiful things together. I hope it inspires group workers to keep doing old-fashioned activity groups. I hope people learn about your lives. I hope people learn from your lives. I hope your families and friends appreciate your stories. I hope someday we can publish an edition with Spanish and English side-by-side—although I'm not sure what to think about a Spanish translation of my English rendering of your Spanish words.

And to my social work colleagues, I say: This book does not report the results of a randomized controlled trial. But does it not serve as evidence of the value of activity-based and arts-based group work? Of dialogic practice? Please accept it as a keepsake of practice based on love, trust, and transparency.

Sharing stories with the four of you is a privilege and a joy. I am looking forward to our party.

## Acknowledgments

The authors would like to thank Christopher Babbitt, Abigail Beckel, Peter Karol, Michelle Singleton, Lyda Vanegas, and Joan Yengo for legal and logistical support related to this project. Thanks also to Michael Sachse and Veronica Suleiman for feedback on the manuscript.

We also extend deep appreciation to Otis College of Art and Design for providing a faculty grant to support the design and production of this publication.

Our love and gratitude go to all the people who make possible the Bernice Fonteneau Senior Wellness Center: the BFSWC team and volunteers; the staff from the DC Office on Aging; the TERRIFIC INC. nutrition and social services staff; and the staff from Mary's Center. Big and very special thanks to Maria Gomez, Ruth Romero, and Michelle Singleton.

## Notes on Design, aka the Colophon

This is the colophon—the brief notation, often found on an otherwise blank page at the very front or very back of a book, that describes details of the production process: the kind of paper used, the name of the typeface, and sometimes the name of its designer. As a book designer I have always loved this part of the book, which pays homage to choices and craft that often get ignored or unnoticed—details that only the trained eye could catch or even be interested in. These details go unnoticed mostly because, more often than not, the book designer is only a invisible presence in the process, there to serve the author, the publisher and the infrastructure of buying and selling books. To highlight these elements of the book is a way to say to the designer, "I see you."

*This* note on design is not about the typeface choices or production references (although you can find those details in the actual colophon of the book on the page opposite the title page). This note is about the design *process*, and the uncertain space between choices and outcomes. For us at Thick Press, design is not about wrapping things up perfectly, or about stripping down an idea so that it is perfectly sterile to the point of invisibility. The design process is not one of matching a straightforward problem with a perfect solution, but rather a messy set of questions to be experienced and celebrated. Our process involves listening, negotiating, understanding, and creating. It honors collaboration, craft, intention, intuition, and trust. It is a space where ego is replaced with vulnerability. Through this process, I have realized that my "presence" feels real when the process is rich. I have felt honored to design the right space for the stories that came from the *Grupo de Cuentos y Memorias*. Serving the authors has never felt this right.

*Julie Cho*

*Image Captions*

p. 49—Jose Lovos (far right) at a catechism class in la Universidad El Castaño de la Vía de Chirilagua, San Miguel, 1980.

p. 53—Jose Lovos in front of the Marriot Wardman Park, one of the Washington, DC properties he maintained, approximately 1985.

p. 56—Jose Lovos at the Bernice Fonteneau Senior Wellness Center, late 2017.

p. 49—Gloria Revelo in Ocean City, MD, 1979.

p. 50—Gloria Revelo visiting her family's farm in Las Lomitas, San Miguel, with her two biological children, 1981. They are standing in front of yucca plants.

p. 51—Gloria Revelo's bible, scanned with the photocopier at the Senior Wellness Center.

p. 52—Gloria Revelo's passports from El Salvador.

p. 53—Gloria Revelo's diplomatic visa.

p. 55—Gloria Revelo is holding five hats that she crocheted, a skill she perfected at the Senior Wellness Center. Every Christmas, she sends hats to St. Jude's Hospital.

p. 56—Gloria Revelo at the Bernice Fonteneau Senior Wellness Center, late 2017.

p. 52—Angela Celaya's identity card from El Salvador.

p. 54—This photo shows Angela Celaya in front of the Great Pyramids of Giza, in Egypt, approximately 2007. As a gift, Angela's employer sent her on a tour of the Middle East. Angela was unable to locate the original of the photo we used for her *Grupo de Cuentos y Memorias* memoir, so we photographed the cover of the memoir itself.

p. 56— Angela Celaya at the Bernice Fonteneau Senior Wellness Center, 2017.

p. 51—During his time with the *Oficinas Sanitarias Panamericanas*, Sergio Guzmán climbed the Volcán de Izalco and descended into the crater. This photo of the volcano appeared in a 2009 calendar that Sergio received from his local market.

p. 54—Sergio Guzmán in Culmore, VA, not long after the attacks of September 11, 2001. At the time, he was working at the Navy Annex.

p. 55—This is a project that Sergio Guzmán made for an English class in 2010. He has fond memories of the class.